REAL BIOS

LIONEL MESSI

By Marie Morreale

Children's Press®
An Imprint of Scholastic Inc.

Photos ©: cover: Jean Catuffe/Getty Images; back cover: Lluis Gene/Getty Images; 1: Marc Atkins/Getty Images; 2, 3: Albert Gea/Landov; 4-5: David Ramos/Getty Images; 6-7: Gustau Nacarino/Landov; 7 left inset: Evrim Aydin/Getty Images; 7 right inset: Reuters/Landov; 8: Javier Heinzmann/Getty Images; 9: Escuela General Las Heras/Getty Images; 11: ZUMA Press, Inc./Alamy Images; 12: Horovitz-Pagni/Newscom; 14: Miquel Benitez/Getty Images; 15 top left: Cosmin Manci/Shutterstock, Inc.; 15 top right: Toshifumi Kitamura/Getty Images; 15 bottom: Manu Fernandez/AP Images; 16: Ververidis Vasilis/Shutterstock, Inc.; 17 top left: Molnia/Dreamstime; 17 top right: Miff32/Dreamstime; 17 center: Neil Lockhart/Shutterstock, Inc.; 17 bottom: Juan Moyano/Dreamstime; 18: Scott Bales/Newscom; 21 top: Daniel Luna/AP Images; 21 bottom: Andreu Dalmau/Newscom; 22: Manu Fernandez/AP Images; 23 top: Lluis Gene/Getty Images; 23 bottom: Manu Fernandez/AP Images; 24 top: David Ramos/Getty Images; 24 bottom: AFP/Getty Images; 25: Paul Hanna/Reuters; 27: A.Pauli/Newscom; 28: Ian MacNicol/Getty Images; 30: Metin Pala/Getty Images; 31: Lluis Gene/Getty Images; 33: David Ramos/Getty Images; 34: Juan Mabromata/Getty Images; 35: Europa Press via Getty Images; 36-41 background: conejota/Thinkstock; 36 pushpins and throughout: seregam/Thinkstock; 36 lined paper and throughout: My Life Graphic/Shutterstock, Inc.; 37 blue paper and throughout: Nonnakrit/Shutterstock, Inc.; 37 top left: Zkruger/Dreamstime; 37 top right: Gabriel Robledo/Dreamstime; 37 bottom: Gonzalo Arroyo Moreno/Getty Images; 38: Peter Kim/Dreamstime; 40 left: Chinafotopress/Newscom; 40 right: Allstar Picture Library/Alamy Images; 41: Lluis Gene/Getty Images; 42: Miguel Ruiz/FC Barcelona via Getty Images; 43: Lluis Gene/Getty Images; 45: Karel Navarro/AP Images.

Library of Congress Cataloging-in-Publication Data
Morreale, Marie.
  Lionel Messi / by Marie Morreale.
    pages cm. — (Real bios)
  Includes bibliographical references and index.
  ISBN 978-0-531-22379-6 (library binding) —
  ISBN 978-0-531-22563-9 (pbk.)
  1. Messi, Lionel, 1987– —Juvenile literature. 2. Soccer play-
ers—Argentina—Biography—Juvenile literatrue. I. Title.
  GV942.7.M398M67 2016
  796.334092—dc23 [B]   2015025188

All rights reserved. Published in 2016 by Children's Press, an imprint of Scholastic Inc.

Printed in the United States 113
SCHOLASTIC, CHILDREN'S PRESS, and associated logos are trademarks and/or registered trademarks of Scholastic Inc.

1 2 3 4 5 6 7 8 9 10 R 25 24 23 22 21 20 19 18 17 16

Leo celebrates another win with his Barcelona teammates.

MEET LEO!

SOCCER'S SENSATIONAL SUPERSTAR!

Lionel "Leo" Messi first set foot on the soccer **pitch** when he was just five years old. Nicknamed the Flea by his older brother Rodrigo, the little tyke was born to play the world's most popular sport. But way back in 1992, no one had a hint that Leo would eventually become the number one player in the world. They knew he was good . . . but he became much more than that! He is also awesome, astounding, and awe-inspiring . . . and that's just the *A* words!

In this *Real Bio*, you will learn about Leo's early days in his hometown of Rosario, Argentina, and his career-changing move to Barcelona, Spain. You will find out how he became an international superstar, but you will also see his other sides: family man, car enthusiast, food fanatic, and more. You will even find out his mom's secret recipe for his favorite meal, *milanesa a la napolitana*! Once you finish this book, you will be yelling "G-O-A-L!"

CONTENTS

Leo executes an overhead play against Nicolás Otamendi of Valencia CF.

THE FLEA JUMPS FROM ARGENTINA TO SPAIN

LEO WAS SMALL AND YOUNG, BUT HE WAS ALREADY A SUPERSTAR

Soccer—also called football or fútbol—is the most popular sport in the world. There are professional soccer teams on six continents: Europe, Asia, North America, Africa, Australia, and South America. It is especially popular in South America, which boasts many of the game's most legendary players, such as Pelé from Brazil and Diego Maradona from Argentina. The same continent is home to today's best player, Leo Messi, who is also from Argentina.

Even before Leo was born, his father, Jorge, mother, Celia, older brothers Matías and Rodrigo, and maternal grandmother, Celia Cuccittini, were huge soccer fans. And when younger sister Maria was born, she joined the soccer fan club, too!

The Messis lived in the city of Rosario, Argentina. Leo's father worked at a steelmaking company, and

Leo adds another scoring ball to his huge collection!

Leo's dad, Jorge, used to coach soccer at the Grandoli club.

Celebration time after Leo scores a goal in a La Liga match against Club Atlético de Madrid.

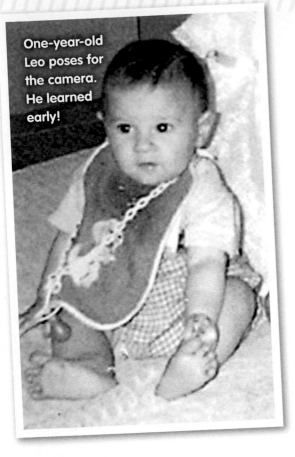

One-year-old Leo poses for the camera. He learned early!

his mother worked at a magnet manufacturing company. They lived in a two-story brick house, which Jorge had built with the help of his father, Eusebio. It had room for their growing family and a backyard so the kids could play outdoors. The Messi house was always full of family, fabulous cooking, and lots of fun. But the one subject that always brought them together was soccer. They loved the game. The kids played it, Jorge coached it, and they all went to watch the local team's matches.

As a child, little Leo was shy. He loved watching his brothers and cousins play soccer, but he spent a lot of his time inside playing marbles. He was small for his age, so his family thought he might have been reluctant to kick a soccer ball around with the bigger boys. Well, that ended when Leo was given a white ball with red diamonds for his fourth birthday. At first, he still didn't join his brothers outside, but he always kept his ball close by. He even slept with it. One day, Matías, Rodrigo, and Jorge were outside playing soccer in the street. Leo hopped in and started making moves. "We were stunned when we saw what he could do," Jorge told Luca Caioli, the author of *Messi: The Inside Story of the Boy Who Became a Legend.* "He had never played before."

Leo must have learned a lot from watching others play soccer, because even at the age of four, people realized he was a whiz kid. "My first memories are from when I was very little, maybe three or four years old, playing in my neighborhood at home," Leo told worldsoccer.com. "I can picture myself with the ball at my feet from a very young age."

At five years old, Leo was in elementary school and already playing soccer!

Leo's biggest fan was his grandmother, Celia, who took care of him and his siblings while his parents were working. She often took Matías and Rodrigo to soccer practice, and Leo tagged along to watch. When Leo was five, he joined one of the local youth soccer clubs, Grandoli. Leo's grandmother often brought him to the Grandoli pitch to watch the games. On the sidelines, Leo would practice kicking a ball against the stands. Grandoli's coach, Salvador Ricardo Aparicio, noticed his skills. Celia often suggested that Aparicio try Leo on the pitch, but he was reluctant because of the boy's small size. But one day, Aparicio needed one more boy to fill out a team of kids born in 1986.

According to author Luca Caioli, Coach Aparicio asked Celia to let Leo play even though the other boys were bigger and one year older. He said, "I'll stand him over here [by the sidelines], and if they attack him, I'll stop the game and take him off." Grandma Celia claims that she was the one who noticed the team was short one boy and urged the coach to play Leo. Aparicio finally agreed, but in this version of the story, he told Celia, "OK, but I'm putting him near the **touch line** so that when he cries you can take him off yourself."

Whichever story you believe, no one was crying by the end of the game. Especially Aparicio. "[Leo] was born in '87 [but] he played with the '86 team," he told Caioli. "He was the smallest in stature and the youngest, but he really stood out. And they punished him hard, but he was a distinctive player, with supernatural talent. He was born knowing how to play. When we would go to a game, people would pile in to see him. When he got the ball he destroyed it. He was unbelievable, they couldn't stop him."

That's why his brother Rodrigo nicknamed him the Flea. On the soccer field, no one could stop Leo. Well, the little Flea had an itch to make a big name for himself. When he was eight years old, Leo moved from Grandoli to Rosario's famed Club Atlético Newell's Old Boys. His father played there, as did both his brothers. The coaches knew all about Leo, and they asked Rodrigo and Matías to bring him in. Leo started trying out with the club's minor leagues right away. After a month of playing different positions and impressing the coaches, he was placed on a team called the 87th Machine.

Leo (front row, second from right) with his Grandoli teammates and coach.

Leo's father, Jorge (left), is very proud of his youngest son.

One of Leo's coaches, Ernesto Vecchio, later said, "He was something special. He had wisdom. He could sprint, his passes were spot on, he played for his teammates, but was capable of going past half the opposing team. Once on the Malvinas first pitch, the goalie passed him the ball in defense and he ran the length of the pitch and went on to score an incredible goal. He didn't need to be taught a thing. What can you teach a Maradona or a Pelé? There are only very tiny things for a coach to correct."

Things were going great. However, Leo's parents began to worry about his size. He was always smaller than the other kids, and he still wasn't growing much at all. When he was nine years old, his parents took him to a doctor to find out if there was anything wrong. Leo went through a series of tests, and it was discovered that his body wasn't producing enough **hormones** for him to grow at a normal rate. The solution was to give him daily injections of the growth hormone for anywhere from three to six years. The treatment worked, and Leo began to get taller and bigger. However, the cost of the medicine soon became too much for the family to afford. Newell's Old Boys stepped in and helped out with the cost for a while. When Leo was 13, however, the club could no longer afford to pay for the injections either. Leo had grown after being on the hormones for several years, but he was still very small— especially for someone with professional soccer dreams.

Just when all looked lost, two businessmen contacted Jorge. They said they could arrange an introduction with the great Spanish soccer team FC Barcelona. If the team was interested in 13-year-old Leo, it might be willing to help pay for his hormone treatments.

Jorge and Leo flew to Spain to meet with the team. They were excited to travel abroad, but they were even more excited about meeting the coaches and players of the team, which was nicknamed Barça. Even though everyone was surprised at how small Leo was, he was allowed to train with Barça's junior team. When Carles Rexach, the team manager, watched the junior team practice, he immediately knew that little Leo Messi had found a new home. Rexach later said, "I said to the coaches: 'We have to sign him. Now.' For what did I see? A kid who was very small but totally different from anyone else. He had incredible confidence, agility, speed, great technique; he could run full speed with the ball, dodging anyone in his way without hesitation. It wasn't difficult to spot; these talents everyone now knows were obvious, even though he was just thirteen years old."

Signing Leo to the team wasn't a simple process. There were problems concerning his age and medical condition. Also, he

FACT FILE

THE BASICS

Home Sweet Home
Leo still owns his childhood home in Rosario.

FULL NAME:
Lionel Andrés Messi

NICKNAME: Leo,
the Flea (La Pulga in
Spanish), the Atomic Flea

BIRTHPLACE: Rosario,
Argentina

BIRTHDATE: June 24, 1987

PARENTS: Celia and Jorge
Messi

SIBLINGS: Older brothers
Rodrigo and Matías,
younger sister, Maria

WIFE: Antonella Roccuzzo

SON: Thiago

ROLE MODEL:
Portuguese soccer
player Cristiano
Ronaldo

Older brother
Rodrigo shows
off one of
Leo's awards.

BIG BREAK: A video of Leo playing got
Barça interested in him

FUN FACT: Leo can sleep 12 hours a
day!

2015 INCOME: $51,800,000, plus
$22,000,000 from **endorsements**

TWITTER HANDLE: @
Messi_Oficial

FACEBOOK: www.facebook
.com/LeoMessi

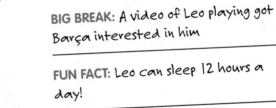

was not a Spanish citizen, and his family would need to move to Spain to be with him. After all these concerns were ironed out, another problem cropped up. Another Spanish team, Real Madrid, was getting interested in Leo. To protect his future superstar, Rexach met with Leo's representatives for a lunch. An agreement was handwritten on a napkin and signed by all. Though it wasn't actually binding, it would do until January 8, 2001, when a real contract was signed. Leo Messi was now an official member of the FC Barcelona family!

FACT FILE

FAVORITES

"MOVING TO BARCELONA FROM ARGENTINA AT 13 WAS THE HARDEST MOMENT IN MY LIFE."

PASTIME: Sleeping

SPORTS: Soccer and handball

ANIMAL: Dog

COLOR: Red

CHILDHOOD GAME: Marbles

DESSERT: Ice cream

VACATION SPOTS: The Spanish island of Ibiza and Sitges beach in South Barcelona

Leo's number 10 uniform is the world's best-selling soccer shirt!

BOOK: "El 'Martin Fierro'" by Jorge Luis Borges

GENRES OF MUSIC: Cumbia and samba

AMUSEMENT PARK: Disneyland

TV SHOWS: "Lost" and "Prison Break"

MOVIES: "Son of the Bride" and "Nine Queens"

Leo was ecstatic when he was named to the 2008 Argentina men's Olympic soccer team.

"WINNING TITLES FOR THE TEAM IS MORE IMPORTANT THAN WINNING INDIVIDUAL AWARDS."

LEO BECOMES
BARCELONA'S
BEST

THE MAKING OF A LEGEND

FC Barcelona is mostly known for its national team, but the efforts of its junior teams are also highly respected. La Masia (the farm) is Barça's youth academy that prepares the younger players. It is right next to Camp Nou, which is Barça's home field. The junior teams learn the ins and outs of soccer. They practice, play, practice, and play again.

Leo thrived at La Masia. He continued to grow, finally reaching a height of five feet seven inches. He also learned real teamwork. "It helped me a lot because I came [from Argentina] alone, and I was with all the guys in the Masia," he told *Time For Kids*. "We were all from someplace else, and we helped each other. The truth is that there were a lot of happy moments because we were there together for a lot of time, and the relationships between all of us got stronger and stronger. Lots of happy times."

As for what he learned on the Masia soccer field, Leo was amazed. "My style of play [had] always been the same," he explained to worldsoccer.com. "I never tried to develop a specific style. From very young I just played this way. What is certainly true is that I learned a lot in the youth system. The way we worked here was different. There was a lot of contact with the ball and a lot of work on the tactical system. I came from Argentina where we didn't do anything like that. Over there it was lots of running and not much more."

Over the next years, some of Leo's mates went off to play for other teams, but he chose to stay with Barça. He felt he owed the team a lot, and he knew he would continue to learn more. Leo played in Barcelona's Juvenil and Cadet teams—sort of like baseball's minor league teams—and achieved an amazing record.

In 2004, Leo was asked to play in the Under-20 World Cup for the Spanish team. Though he had come to love

Leo's Timeline

Leo's Goals Come True!

1992
Five-year-old Leo joins the Grandoli soccer club in Rosario, Argentina

1995
Leo moves to Rosario's top soccer club, Newell's Old Boys

JANUARY 31, 1997
Leo is diagnosed with growth hormone deficiency

his new home of Spain, he instead chose to play for the Argentina team—which turned out to be a very good move. Argentina won the FIFA World Youth Championship, and Leo was given the Golden Ball for best player and the Golden Shoe for being the top scorer in the games.

When Leo was 16, he played with Barcelona's senior team in an **exhibition game**. Almost a year later, he reached his longtime goal: he debuted on Barcelona's main team in a La Liga game against the

Though usually quiet, Leo has learned how to be interviewed by the press.

SEPTEMBER 16, 2000
Leo and his father leave Rosario for Barcelona to try out for FC Barcelona

JANUARY 8, 2001
Leo is signed by FC Barcelona and starts in the junior leagues

OCTOBER 16, 2004
Leo makes his debut with Barça's main team

Spanish team Espanyol. La Liga is the top division of Spain's professional soccer league. The next months were spectacular for him. He played in his first European Champions League game against the Ukraine's FC Shakhtar.

Leo was also thrilled when he scored his first goal during a home game at Camp Nou. Over the following years, Leo scored goal after goal and helped win game after game and title after title. Diego Maradona, a soccer legend and fellow Argentinian, told the *China Daily*, "I have seen the player who will inherit my place in . . . football and his name is Messi."

In the beginning, living, studying, and playing in Spain was quite an experience for Leo and his family. So much was happening that it almost was overwhelming, but Leo kept to the program, worked hard, and learned new things. One thing he learned was how to work

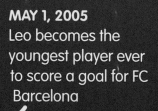

MAY 1, 2005
Leo becomes the youngest player ever to score a goal for FC Barcelona

MAY 15, 2006
Leo is named to the Argentina World Cup team

AUGUST 23, 2008
At the Summer Olympics, Leo and the Argentina team win the gold medal

DECEMBER 2009
Leo wins his first FIFA World Player of the Year award—the Ballon d'Or

Training time at the Camp Nou stadium for Leo and his teammates

with a team—not only on the pitch but also in day-to-day activity. Leo explained a typical training day to *FourFourTwo*. "We all arrive an hour before training starts," he said. "We all have breakfast together when we arrive, then everyone goes about their own business before the football starts. Some will go into the gym for

MARCH 2010
Leo becomes a UNICEF goodwill ambassador

APRIL 21, 2011
Leo is named one of *Time* magazine's 100 Most Influential People

Leo and teammate Andrés Iniesta cheer after wining yet another match!

half an hour to prepare themselves; others will see the physio [physical therapist] for a stretch, especially if they have a small injury complaint. There's a group of us who have *mate* [a type of tea] together before training starts. Sometimes I'll go for a wander

2012
Leo sets a record by scoring 91 goals in 69 games

JANUARY 7, 2012
Leo becomes the first player ever to win the FIFA Ballon d'Or award four years in a row

NOVEMBER 20, 2013
Leo and Antonella marry in Ibiza

around the training ground or sit in the dressing room. It all depends on each day, really, but the *mate* and having a chat with my teammates I'll do every day. We arrive, have a drink and a chat. There isn't a reason why, it's just what we've always done."

Leo's talent, dedication, and teamwork led Barcelona to extend his contract to 2018. Leo has said that he hopes to play for Barça until he retires.

In 2006, Leo made his first appearance on the international field. He was a member of the 2006 Argentina World Cup team. An injury kept him out of some of the early games. He first took the field in a game against Serbia, where he scored the final goal, giving Argentina a 6–0 win. He was the youngest player in the tournament to score a goal. Unfortunately, Argentina lost in the quarterfinal match against Germany. However, there would be more opportunities to come for Leo.

JUNE 12, 2014
Leo is the captain of the Argentina squad for the 2014 World Cup

APRIL 18, 2015
Leo scores his 400th goal for Barcelona

In the 2008 Summer Olympics in Beijing, China, Leo played for Argentina's squad. He scored the first goal in Argentina's victory over the Côte d'Ivoire team. On August 23, Leo and his teammates beat Nigeria to win the gold medal.

In 2010, Leo again joined the Argentina team for the World Cup. He was nominated for the Golden Ball award but didn't win it. Argentina once again lost to Germany in the quarterfinals.

The 2014 World Cup was a big tournament for Leo. He was captain of Argentina's team. He also won four Man of the Match awards and the Golden Ball award. He was even named to the FIFA World Cup All-Star Team. Unfortunately, Argentina lost 1–0 to its old nemesis, Germany, in the finals of the World Cup.

Though disappointed that he has been unable so far to lead Argentina to a World Cup victory, Leo is not one to give in to defeat. He maintains that he is still learning and getting better—even though the soccer world already considers him the best player ever. He will continue to give his all to Barcelona and to the Argentina national team.

Leo has also found great success in his personal life. He and his wife, Antonella Roccuzzo, grew up together in Rosario—they have known each other since they were five years old. Antonella is the cousin of one of

Leo's good friends. Over the years, their friendship turned to romance and love. They have a young son named Thiago, and he is daddy's little boy. One of Thiago's first presents was an official FC Barcelona shirt. Leo and Antonella are happiest when they are together with their son. "I go home, I say that I have scored two or three goals and she doesn't hear me," Leo laughingly told messinews.net. "And I go watch cartoons with Thiago, and he laughs a lot."

Sounds like Leo Messi has already won life's gold cup!

Leo and his wife, Antonella, dress up for a night on the town.

"YOU HAVE TO FIGHT TO REACH YOUR DREAM. YOU HAVE TO SACRIFICE AND WORK HARD FOR IT."

Leo waves to fans as they cheer their hero!

FANS ASK . . . LEO ANSWERS

LEO REVEALS WHAT HE LOVES AND WHAT MAKES HIM LAUGH!

He's been declared the best soccer player of all time. He was named to *Time*'s list of the world's 100 Most Influential People in 2011. More kids wear his soccer jersey than any other. Leo Messi is definitely a superstar. But his interviews show another side to him. He's still the boy next door!

On his success . . . "Every time I start a year, I start with the objective of trying to achieve everything, without comparing it to how I've done in other seasons, to what I've accomplished before, or to what we've accomplished as a group. For me, what's happened has happened, and I'm always looking toward what's ahead. You don't have to stop and think about everything that happens, it all happens too quickly. When I retire, I'll stop and think about that."

Showing off his signature moves, Leo charges down the pitch.

On going out and partying . . . "Ever since I was young, I've always really just liked football, and I've always devoted a lot of time to it. When I was a kid, my friends would call me to go out with them, but I would stay home because I had practice the next day. I like going out, but you have to know when you can and when you can't. That's why I say nothing's changed since I was young."

FLEA
Leo never let being small bother him.

On being small . . . "I never had any problems with my height. I was always the smallest kid, at school and in my teams."

On preparing for a game . . . "I start preparing for a game, much like the rest of the squad, after the previous match finishes. We talk about what we did well and what we can improve. We play a lot of games in a very short space of time, so I think it's important to always look forward and never backwards in football. . . . I'm not the sort of guy who goes around shouting and

Before a game starts, Leo imagines what his opponents might do.

screaming in the dressing room before a game, either. I prefer to stay calm, be with my own thoughts and think about some of the situations that I'm likely to face in the upcoming game."

On how he relaxes . . . "I don't play other sports. I enjoy following them on TV, but that's about it. Sometimes I play *FIFA* on the PlayStation against my Barcelona or Argentina teammates, which is always good fun. I wouldn't say I'm the king, though, there are a few who are pretty good."

On why he loves meeting young fans . . . "Children are pure, especially when they're young. They see you and they transform. Some of them are shy. . . . I'm most fulfilled when I make a child happy."

On not being a hater . . . "I'm not looking for problems or conflicts. I don't see the point in saying bad things about people you don't know at all. I prefer to be respectful to others, nothing more."

On being the highest-paid soccer player in the world . . . "Money is not a motivating factor for me. It does not make me a better player. I would play for nothing willingly."

On how he takes a loss . . . "I am competitive and I feel bad when we lose. You can see it in me when we've lost. I'm in a bad way. I don't like to talk to anyone. I just retreat into myself and go over the game in my head: the things that went wrong, what I did wrong, why we didn't win."

On how he feels about his fans all over the world . . . "Incredible. [I've had a good reception] in a lot of countries I've visited, but it's still surprising. I never imagined that so far from Spain or Argentina, people would have this affection for me. It makes me very happy."

Argentina's World Cup coach Diego Maradona goes over plays with Leo.

On the advice he got from soccer icon Diego Maradona . . . "He told me to keep doing what I'm doing, always to enjoy football and to look after myself, because it's a short career and if you want to improve throughout it and make it last as long as possible, you always have to be in good shape."

On being on the Argentina World Cup team . . . "Wearing the national shirt is something really great. Although I live thousands of miles away, I would like to be at all the games and bring a lot of happiness to my people."

On Thiago understanding his dad is a superstar . . .

"Honestly right now not so much because he is still very young, he doesn't understand . . . when he grows up a little bit more he will realize things, where he comes from, where we come from, where we live now and all that stuff. He goes to Argentina a lot, same as me and Antonella."

"Pressure helps me do things to the best of my ability."

Leo loves to bring his son, Thiago, to his games.

LEO'S SCOREBOARD

FUN 'N' FAST FACTS . . . FAVES 'N' FIRSTS!

THE NAME GAME

BIRTH NAME:
LIONEL ANDRÉS MESSI

NAME CHANGE
ORIGINALLY LEO'S DAD WANTED TO SPELL "LIONEL" WITH AN E—"LEONEL"—BUT THOUGHT "LIONEL" LOOKED BETTER

MYTH
LEO WAS NOT NAMED AFTER AMERICAN SINGER LIONEL RICHIE

MEANING
LIONEL MEANS "LITTLE LION"

FOODIE HEAVEN

MOM'S SPECIAL DINNER
MILANESA A LA NAPOLITANA

DRINK
MATE (A TYPE OF TEA)

SEAFOOD
SCALLOPS

CANDY
DULCE DE LECHE (A SWEET TREAT MADE OF MILK AND SUGAR)

MEAT
STEAK

SANDWICH
CHICKEN SALAD

BAKERY TREATS
ALFAJORES (CARAMEL-FILLED BISCUITS)

FANTASTIC FIRSTS

- Leo is the first soccer player to win four consecutive FIFA Ballon d'Or awards.
- For his first birthday, Leo's aunts and uncles bought him a Newell's Old Boys football shirt.
- Leo got his first brand-new adult size soccer ball for his fourth birthday.
- Grandoli was Leo's first youth team—he was five years old when he joined.
- Leo's first time on the pitch for Argentina's national team lasted only 40 seconds!

CELIA MESSI'S MILANESA A LA NAPOLITANA RECIPE

"I buy the rump or a piece of hindquarter [of beef]. . . . I put a bit of salt on each piece, dip them in egg and coat them with breadcrumbs. I fry them in an oven dish. I slice the onion finely and fry it over. When the onion turns white, I add chopped tomatoes, a little water, salt, oregano and a pinch of sugar. Once the sauce is done, I pour it on top of each piece of beef, making sure they're well covered. I take some cream cheese or hard cheese out of the fridge and lay it on top of the beef in thin slices. I leave them in the oven until the cheese melts. All that's left to do is fry the potatoes as a side dish and the *milanesa a la napolitana* is ready to serve."

"A CHILD'S SMILE IS WORTH MORE THAN ALL THE MONEY IN THE WORLD."

FIRST INTERVIEW

The year 2000 was the last year Leo played with Newell's Old Boys club. Of course, they won the championship. The Argentina newspaper *La Capital* ran an interview with 13-year-old Leo. Part of it included this list:

IDOLS
MY FATHER AND MY GRANDFATHER, CLAUDIO

AIMS
TO MAKE IT INTO THE FIRST TEAM

FAVORITE PLAYERS
MY BROTHER AND MY COUSIN

HAPPIEST MOMENT
WHEN WE BECAME CHAMPIONS OF THE TENTH LEAGUE

FAVORITE TEAM
NEWELL'S

SADDEST MOMENT
WHEN MY GRANDMOTHER PASSED AWAY

HOBBY
LISTENING TO MUSIC

FAVORITE BOOK
THE BIBLE

A DREAM
TO PLAY IN THE NEWELL'S FIRST TEAM

FAVORITE FILM
BABY'S DAY OUT

A MEMORY
WHEN MY GRANDMOTHER FIRST TOOK ME TO PLAY FOOTBALL

FAVORITE TEACHER
PE TEACHER

OBJECTIVES
TO FINISH SECONDARY SCHOOL

HUMILITY
IS SOMETHING A HUMAN BEING SHOULD NEVER LOSE

CARS, CARS & MORE CARS

Leo is known to be speedy on the soccer field, but he also loves the feeling of the wind in his face while driving one of his amazing cars. Check out what's parked in front of his house right now. Of course, Leo is always making new additions to the collection!

- Maserati GranTurismo MC Stradale
- Maserati GranTurismo S
- Lexus 4x4
- Dodge Charger SRT8
- Audi Q7
- Ferrari F430 Spider
- Audi R8 Spyder

Maserati GranTurismo MC Stradale

Ferrari F430 Spider

FUN STUFF

- When Leo scores, he always raises two fingers to the sky to honor his late grandmother.
- Both Jorge and Celia Messi's families originally came from Italy.
- At the age of 25, Leo became the youngest player to score 200 goals in La Liga games.
- Leo has the Guinness World Record for scoring the most goals in a year.
- Leo never watches films or video of his highlights.
- When Leo was asked to play for the Argentina Under-20 national team, officials misspelled his name—Leonel Mecci—in the letter.
- Leo claims he's not superstitious, but he always plays with wet hair!

DREAMS
DO COME TRUE
A LIFETIME OF LOVE!

"Lifting a title makes me feel so happy because it's what I want to do in football: be successful," Leo told *FourFourTwo*. "I find it impossible to single out specific victories, because they all mean so much to me. The Champions League is the best tournament there is, but the enjoyment I feel from winning any trophy is very special. When I was a kid, playing in the streets of Rosario, I'd never have imagined that I'd have reached the level I have and won Ligas, Champions League, and other very important titles. I didn't even imagine that I'd be living in Spain, or playing for a professional club as huge as Barcelona, let alone anything else. That all seemed a long way away for us as a family, but it's exactly what's happened. It's amazing."

What is also amazing is that Leo has achieved so much in his personal life, too. He married his longtime love, Antonella, and they had little Thiago. Always the devoted family man, Leo loves spending time at home with his wife and son, and you better believe he is teaching Thiago some fancy moves. Thiago is already an "official" member of Newell's Old Boys Club. Leo laughed with a reporter from metro951, "I think he's a member of many clubs and he doesn't even know . . . many clubs sent him shirts and member cards."

WHEN THIAGO IS OFFERED A BALL OR SOME OTHER TOY, LEO SAYS HE "ALWAYS CHOOSES THE BALL!"

Family fun—Antonella, Leo, and Thiago are the picture of happiness.

You can be sure that little Thiago will have the best of coaches if he wants to follow in his father's footsteps. But Leo is also clear that if his son wants to do something else, he would support him 100 percent.

Leo's love of children is well known. In 2007, he started the Leo Messi Foundation, which provides education and health care for needy children. One of its missions is to help children whose families can't afford the cost of medical services. The foundation has helped seriously ill Argentinian kids travel to Spain for medical treatment, just like Leo did many years ago. As an ambassador for UNICEF, Leo has participated in charity campaigns for kids all across the world. He has also donated money closer to home by helping rebuild the children's hospital in Rosario and setting up a fund for the hospital's doctors to study in Barcelona.

In 2015, Leo joined tennis icon Serena Williams in the "1 in 11" campaign. The campaign is named for the number of children worldwide who can't go to school. It is very important to Leo. He explained, "I'm supporting the 1 in 11 campaign because I believe every child has the right to fulfill their potential and realize their dreams. Education is fundamental to this, but millions of children across the world are out of school and not getting the start in life they are entitled to. I believe that through sport we can teach values of respect, teamwork, and effort, and ultimately inspire children to attend and stay on in school, so they will receive the quality education which will equip them with the skills they need for life."

Leo wants to give back, not only to those who helped him, but also to those who need his help now and in the future. He knows that while soccer is his love now, it won't be forever. "I'm more concerned with being a good person than being the best footballer in the world . . . My hope is that when I retire that I'm remembered as a good guy."

He will be . . . he definitely will be.

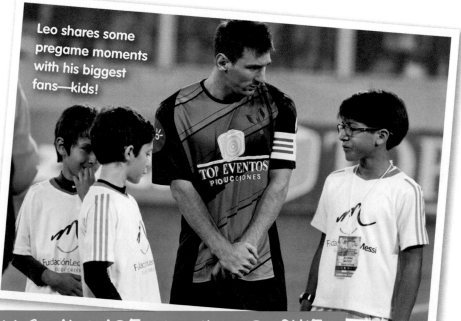

Leo shares some pregame moments with his biggest fans—kids!

"MY GOALS ARE TO WIN TROPHIES AND ACHIEVE EVERYTHING THAT WE POSSIBLY CAN WITH THIS TEAM."

Resources

BOOKS

Caioli, Luca. *Messi: The Inside Story of the Boy Who Became a Legend.* Mt. Pleasant, SC: Corinthian Books, 2013.

Jökulsson, Illugi. *Messi.* New York, NY: Abbeville Kids, 2015.

Part, Michael. *The Flea—The Amazing Story of Leo Messi.* Beverly Hills, CA: Sole Books, 2013.

Perez, Mike. *Lionel Messi: The Ultimate Fan Book.* London, England: Carlton Publishing Group, 2013.

Facts for Now

Visit this Scholastic Web site for more information on **Lionel Messi**: www.factsfornow.scholastic.com
Enter the keywords **Lionel Messi**

Glossary

endorsements *(en-DORS-muhnts)* support or approval of someone or something; famous people are often paid to endorse products

exhibition game *(ek-suh-BISH-uhn GAME)* a friendly athletic competition where there is nothing at stake

hormones *(HOR-mohnz)* chemical substances made by the body that affect the way it grows, develops, and functions

pitch *(PICH)* soccer field

touch line *(TUCH LINE)* a line that marks the boundaries of a soccer pitch

Index

Acknowledgments

Page 9: First soccer game with family: *Messi: The Inside Story of the Boy Who Became a Legend*, 2012

Page 9: First soccer memory: worldsoccer.com May 7, 2015

Page 10: First game for Grandoli: *Messi: The Inside Story of the Boy Who Became a Legend*, 2012

Page 10: Coach Aparicio on Leo: *Messi: The Inside Story of the Boy Who Became a Legend*, 2012

Page 12: Coach Vecchio on Leo: *Messi: The Inside Story of the Boy Who Became a Legend*, 2012

Pages 13–14: Carles Rexach on Leo: *World Soccer Legends: Messi*, 2014

Page 16: Moving to Barcelona: hubpages.com January 10, 2015

Page 18: Winning titles: hubpages.com January 10, 2015

Page 19: Teamwork: *Time For Kids* February 23, 2012

Page 20: Style of play: worldsoccer.com May 7, 2015

Page 22: Diego Maradona on Leo: *China Daily* February 25, 2006

Page 23: Training: *FourFourTwo* April 21, 2015

Page 24: Proud Papa: *FourFourTwo* April 21, 2015

Page 27: Leo on his wife and son: messinews.net

Page 27: Fight to reach your dream: brainyquote.com February 2015

Page 29: On his success: content.time.com January 26, 2012

Page 30: On partying: content.time.com January 26, 2012

Page 30: On being bullied: worldsoccer.com May 7, 2015

Page 31: On preparing for a game: *FourFourTwo* April 21, 2015

Page 32: On how he relaxes: *FourFourTwo* April 21, 2015

Page 32: On young fans: *El País* October 1, 2012

Page 32: On not being a hater: *El País* October 1, 2012

Page 32: On being highest paid player: villyvacker.hubpages.com January 10, 2015

Page 33: On losing: *Time For Kids* February 23, 2012

Page 33: On fans all over the world: *Time For Kids* February 23, 2012

Page 34: On advice from Maradona: *Messi: The Inside Story of the Boy Who Became a Legend*, 2012

Page 34: On being on Argentina World Cup team: *Messi: The Inside Story of the Boy Who Became a Legend*, 2012

Page 35: On Thiago knowing his dad is a star: facebook.com Leo Messi interview with metro951 November 23, 2013

Page 38: Celia Messi's recipe: *Messi: The Inside Story of the Boy Who Became A Legend*, 2012

Page 38: Child's smile: lionelmessibarcelonafc.blogspot.com March 18, 2013

Page 39: First interview: *Messi: The Inside Story of the Boy Who Became a Legend*, 2012

Page 41: Part of a great team: www.brainyquote.com/quotes/quotes/l/lionelmess553568.html

Page 42: Lifting a title: *FourFourTwo* April 15, 2015

Page 43: Thiago and soccer clubs: metro951 November 23, 2013

Page 44: 1 in 11: DailyMail.co.uk June 21, 2015

Page 45: Goals: *FourFourTwo* April 15, 2015

About the Author

Marie Morreale is the author of many official and unofficial celebrity biographies. She attended New York University as an English/creative writing major and began her writing and editorial career in New York City. As the editor of teen/music magazines *Teen Machine* and *Jam!*, she covered TV, film, and music personalities and interviewed superstars such as Michael Jackson, Britney Spears, and Justin Timberlake/*NSYNC. Morreale was also an editor/writer at Little Golden Books.

Today, she is the executive editor, media, of Scholastic Classroom Magazines and writes about pop culture, sports, news, and special events. Morreale lives in New York City and is entertained daily by her two Maine coon cats, Cher and Sullivan.